connecting to universal energies
a collection of haiku

Joshua Roi Keeler

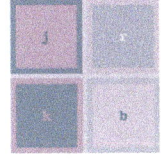

JRK Books
Santa Fe, New Mexico

Copyright ©2024 Joshua Roi Keeler / JRK Books

All rights reserved. In accordance with the U.S. Copyright Act of 1976, the scanning, uploading, and electronic sharing of any part of this book without the permission of the author and publisher constitute unlawful piracy and theft of the intellectual property. If you would like to use material from the book (other than for review purposes), prior written permission must be obtained by contacting the author and publisher at jrkb.publishing@gmail.com. Thank you for your support of the author's rights.

ISBN: 979-8-9908082-0-1 paperback

JRK Books
3201 Zafarano Dr. Ste. C296
Santa Fe, NM 87507

Cover images by Josh Keeler.
Book design by Josh Keeler.

First edition 2024.

for friends,
for walks,
for you

1

like midday ripples
over ponds, hot mirages
play on asphalt hills.

2

rare angry sky tears
apart; shattered stars of ice
jackhammer dirt skin.

3

trenches block her path —
screaming yellow behemoths
have made man master.

4

take the arroyo,
water's curated fury,
an unbeaten path.

5

a dandelion . . .
why have anything at all —
everything must go.

6

bed of pine needles,
cozy refuge of spiders —
painful underfoot.

7

tiny tin tinkles
turn to thunks of pounding rain —
is this a drought year?

8

confining compost
in composite containers —
garden flourishes.

9

a blasted surface —
heaving, propellant, crashing
fluke of majesty.

10

up to fourteen days
your snug petals radiate,
lost cherry blossoms.

11

duet of hatchlings —
a thrumming nearby; am I
to meet the parents?

12

unmovable stone —
an invite to the pickaxe —
be small, be broken.

13

hardware cloth protects
underneath garden heirlooms —
gopher finds a way.

14

stiff legs when threatened,
gaseous pinacate
stakes its desert ground.

15

delightful spring breeze
stirring juniper trees like
whispers of desire.

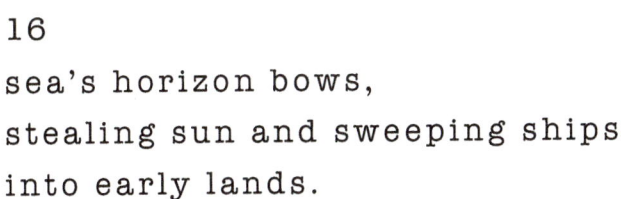

16

sea's horizon bows,
stealing sun and sweeping ships
into early lands.

17

creosote bushes
grease humid air, promising
an evening deluge.

18

waxen wings be damned —
here sun lays its lips on all,
even the grounded.

19

are your insides carved
under fleshy sheaths of bark?
show us why you weep.

20

pebble harvesters,
founders on denuded land —
are we an earthquake?

21

fertility bed
rotates as spring emerges —
a garden's feng shui.

22
I trust my prodding
made no impression upon
young, innocent roots.

23
curiosity
brings us closer together,
like mice sniffing cheese.

24
haze-veiled mountaintop —
barren or bursting with white
in the morning light.

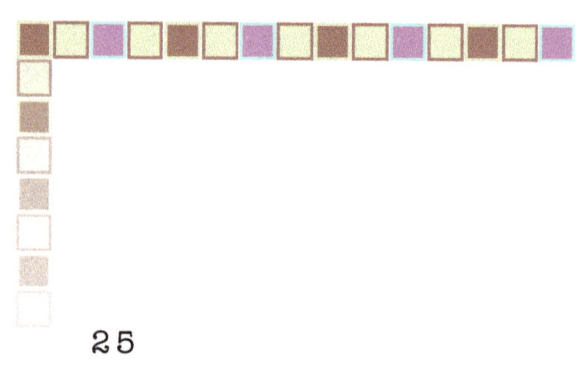

25

breeze before the storm —
dust and seed swirl on blacktop,
transferring secrets.

26

unscalable wall
of boulder, watch as we fall
like enthused water.

27

sweet desert locust
dances in spring — vigorous
tango of nectar.

28

these factured leaves feed
the understory's base like
faded memories.

29

sassy marigold,
stand guard at this bed's corner —
be our protector.

30

to kill a spider,
crush its body on a wall
after the sun sets.

31

when the well is parched,
dry as a horse's salt lick,
where then will we be?

32

the flower unfurls
its infant limbs in hunger,
reaching for the sun.

33

a gravel driveway
painted rough with erosion —
is this memory?

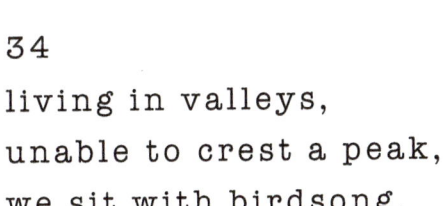

34

living in valleys,
unable to crest a peak,
we sit with birdsong.

35

like blinding white sand,
are we irredeemable
when the light shines down?

36

reflect on color
when the rain clears at sunset:
an alla prima.

37

prismatic droplets
burst with pride as morphing lights
vanish over hills.

38

cumulonimbus
grumbles in disapproval
as we search for stars.

39

serrated mountain,
chipped with age and tectonic
battle scars: you win.

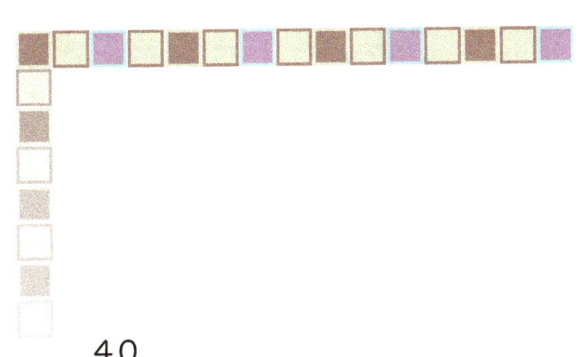

40

not everything sleeps
in the earth's shadow; its chill
thrives with glinted eyes.

41

finches in the pine,
hopping limb to limb, each one
twittering louder.

42

the crickets' chirrups
waft through an open window —
a rasped lullaby.

43

little birds lighted,
provoking the chittering
cat at the window.

44

I skim the koi pond;
pockets of pollen fall in;
I skim it again.

45

radiant lipstick
shades of rose help to forget
nagging mosquitos.

46

a patch of loose dirt
burdened by footprints of which
some may not return.

47

egg cracked on flagstone —
a feud among families?
I heard arguing.

48

your home in rafters —
twigs woven into safety —
you don't want us here.

49

there's something out there —
it's feeding in the darkness,
killing shoots of grass.

50

spreading like ink blots,
smoke signals the ash to come —
savage renewal.

51

decaying cholla —
fingers in the summer dust
grasping for purchase.

52

we are the desert —
dead for thirst yet undrinking —
used to little rain.

53

beelzebub roams —
swelling in concert with wind —
quick stints of chaos.

54

fighting toward calm,
clouds bellow at each other —
spring leaves torn from trees.

55

it's ok to find —
like wind, changing direction —
new destinations.

56

a cracked carapace —
home to the forgotten past —
brittle cast of self.

57

rain skirts around us —
drenched kisses eluding earth
like reserved romance.

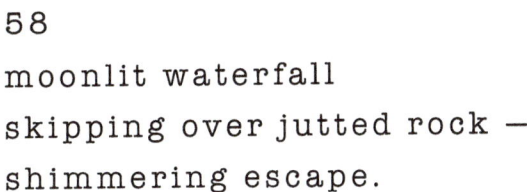

58

moonlit waterfall
skipping over jutted rock —
shimmering escape.

59

pale open petals —
anther quivers with pollen —
summer bee delights.

60

the dog dispels all,
shaking off dislodged nuisance —
the art of shedding.

61

freeing of the tongue:
crow clings to windblown branch,
telling us to run.

62

when the air goes mute
yet screaming walls surround us —
where do the birds go?

63

addicted to light,
drunk moth stumbles at the door —
desire to get home.

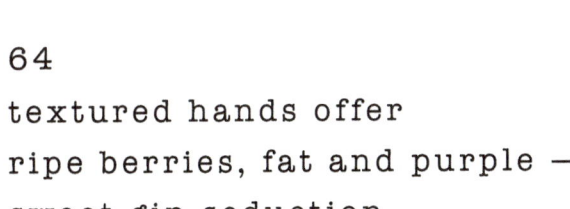

64

textured hands offer
ripe berries, fat and purple —
sweet gin seduction.

65

tattoo on skylight —
a deluge shouts its story
in beaded language.

66

painted gray on green —
a weighted, nurturing load —
the mountain's blanket.

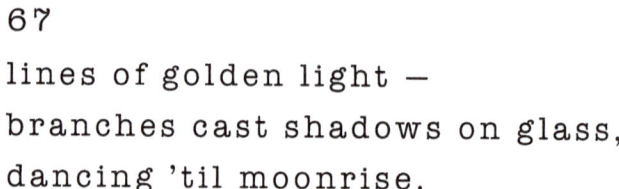

67

lines of golden light —
branches cast shadows on glass,
dancing 'til moonrise.

68

feathers splitting ground —
wild growth gripping hard to life
when none thought you could.

69

roots fused together —
a charged embrace alive like
aortic throbbing.

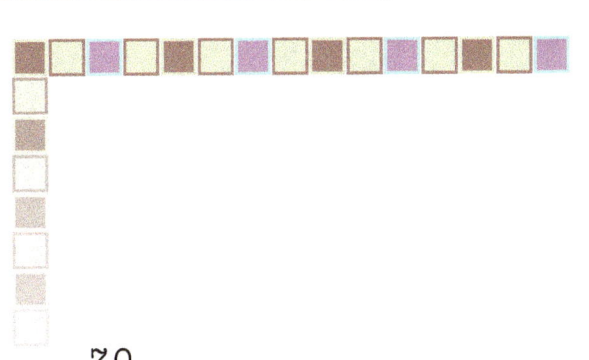

70

walking with magic —
lavender blooms at bare feet
on quieting steps.

71

crops grow in silence,
each millimeter signing
peace to the garden.

72

fingers dig shallow —
soaked soil holds slippery bean —
soon yields rhapsody.

73

riding the storm's edge —
whatever brings us closer
to thunderous bliss.

74

cottonwoods let loose —
fingertips across the face
passing through windows.

75

lying under oak —
branches laden with acorns —
wait for them to fall.

76
like hot scattered sand —
grains orbiting galaxies
on reversed lightbox.

77
swallow swallowed whole —
lost to pooling yellow light —
faded silhouette.

78
opportunity
whenever you face the sun —
seeds grinning, black teeth.

79

timid scorpions
hiding in the sage bushes —
crawling ghosts at night.

80

sun sets smoke ablaze —
a fat, orange orb, smug, cloaked —
one can stare you down.

81

it's only one strike —
dry tree splinters in a flash —
no containing flames.

82

stick with it, honey —
thick glaze on those bent knuckles —
catch dust and laughter.

83

gravel driveway yawns,
waking to garish headlights —
trees stretching like fangs.

84

grass like strands of hair
growing long above graveyards
in memoriam.

85

we may find release
in the most dangerous place —
fish thrashing on land.

86

silver corona ...
clouds peel away like dead skin,
revealing craters.

87

boulders like swiss cheese
wish the stones to levitate —
get caught in their sieve.

88

if we kiss the soil,
eyes closed 'cause it's our last time,
I want you to know—

89

plucking tomatoes,
we reach around fuzzy stalk —
twisting the obscurred.

90

voluptuous laze —
like lizard's peace in sunbeams —
lying on cowhide.

91

I lean like I'm trees —
forced parralel to inclines,
my crown to the clouds.

92

creating heirlooms —
sifting through varietals —
willing sacrifice.

93

searching for that tree —
no black streaks on the concrete —
grass flat: the last sleep.

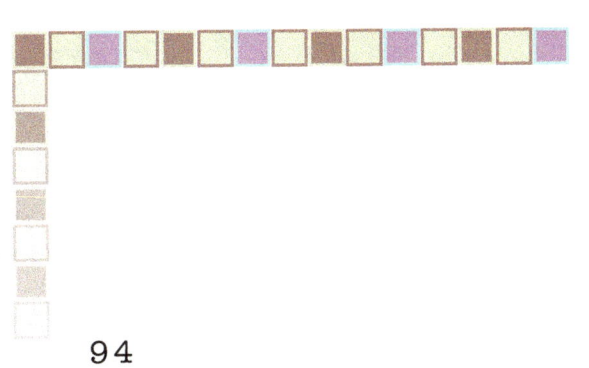

94

salute the summer —
standing as a tamarack —
and season with fall.

95

there is a slug school
hiding among sweet, red rounds —
they learn salt and slime.

96

gray cloud descending —
rind caving in — oozing guts
feed and grow the new.

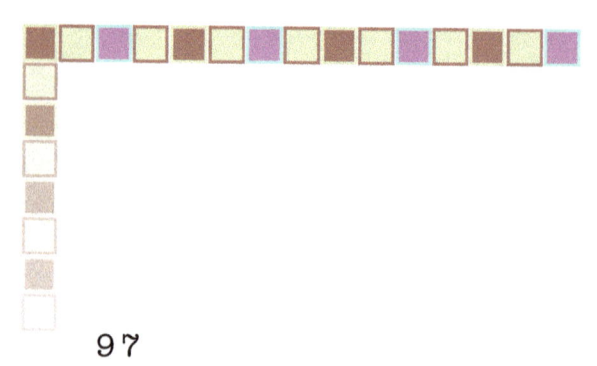

97

I called you magpie —
black bill banked, eye cocked, head bronze —
and you searched for gold.

98

my head sacked with rock
and melted frost on my brow —
a chipped gem vision.

99

small paws on the shelves,
prowling snout, holes in the bags —
a mouse trapped gets zapped.

100

clouds from low are hard,
set, white, gray, and then inside,
blurred blue ludic wisps.

101

they watch from the shade
as seed kin drink and soak sun —
and it's not just place.

102

some cut grass with force —
blades scream, bodies fly — and I
slice each like secrets.

103

stilled by wafts of stock —
honey hugs tongue a moment —
we wait 'til it dulls.

104

when you lost your roots —
flesh and bone cut by dry breath —
you caught wind and flew.

105

it may be the cage,
and just yips and yowls ring night —
pup yearns for less change.

106

hot zinnia break —
flash that red skirt and give birth —
evolving the seed.

107

we are cracked and baked —
the lake is already drained —
no sustenance here.

108

tough to talk with stone —
stuck, chipped smile rigged up like clock —
I've no moss for rock.

109

a tree feels no rage —
loving us is tortuous —
feel like we don't feel.

110

you are swept past us —
brutal bursts of wind rip hair —
there's no closed window.

111

almond beak, black gleam;
I hold nuts, outstretched, thrown close —
lift off, no ... come back.

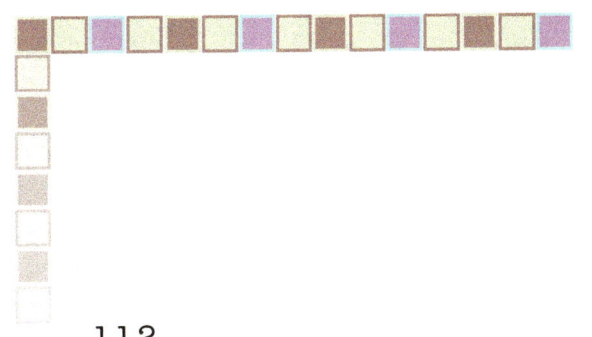

112

cold matte on windshield —
trails of early morning dew
leap to sleeping grass.

113

light soars in dark sky —
rains down in green sheets and swims
to deep sea like squid.

114

sea heats sand to melt —
a kiln keen to turn tan clear —
cools in glassy waves.

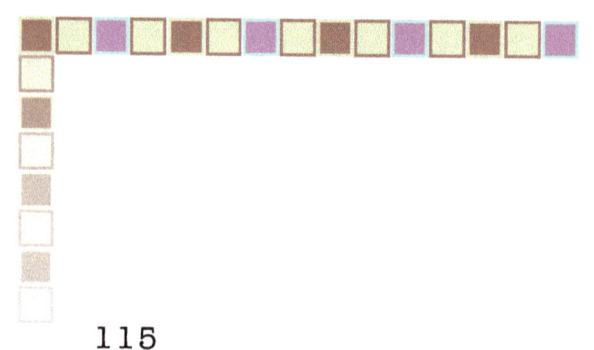

115

a beetle's city:
walled-in curved roads, bowed towers
heavy with promise.

116

dense musk deep in woods
has a deer drawn to his dance,
his sight set on spoil.

117

front bed flower heads —
catch their faces as they rise —
please do not deprive.

118

hide fast 'fore dark falls —
your shell, your wings, your eyes fail —
shocked by wall, by light.

119

foreign hairy lumps
line the tarmac — what are these
many shades of green.

120

spined vine-like tail whips
against palm bark, drips down side —
look up! a dead frond.

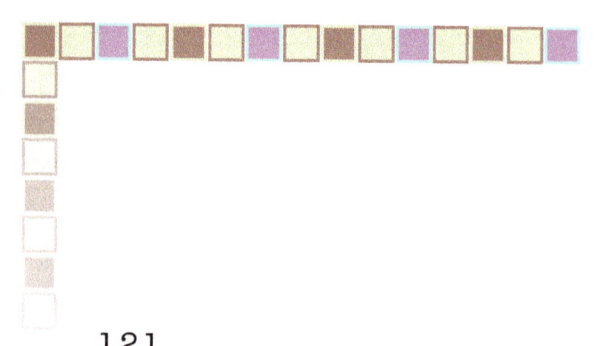

121

heads bowed, groaning wet —
board slick, rail swollen, light fogged —
trudge through paradise.

122

dirt glows thick with sweat —
grime climbing down our faces
as we sift archives.

123

I don't know your name,
but you came at fruit's first sight —
sneaking in for plums.

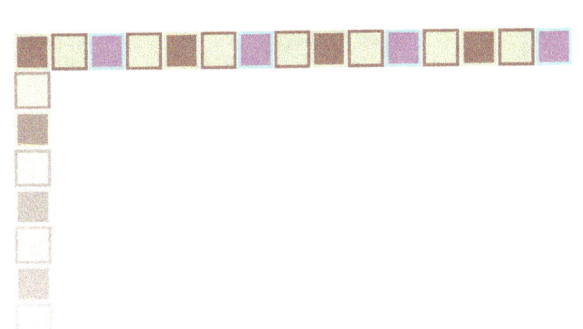

124

a gray scaled monster
tossing sand with each claw prod
finds shade 'neath chaired fiends.

125

we're drenched in hot rain —
magma poured over eyelids —
yet still we're unclean.

126

she's back and it's home —
not because she left it so,
twigs jigged, uplifted.

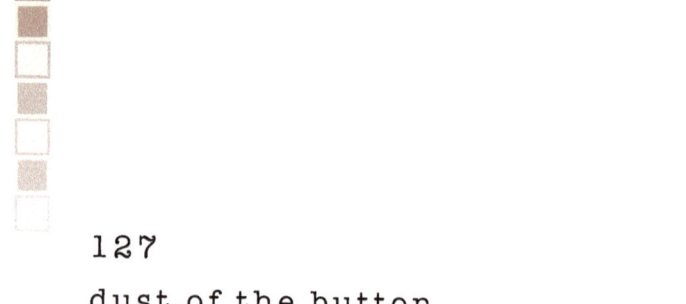

127

dust of the button
breathes waves to the grass, shifting
our minds to receive.

128

you pull in angles,
rounds glisten like record braille
as you spin your web.

129

this cat feels our pain —
tail twitched, paws brushed against death,
and quieting purrs.

130

let the window down —
rain sprays in, settles on knee —
swept to petrichor.

131

you've grown in a sack,
dwelling damp, dark in the dirt —
root tubers to the sun.

132

stunned, slapped from the sky —
fly's wings, legs stiff in a sham —
angor animi?

133

set up on stocked legs —
dozens thrusting deep in earth —
buried by fine limbs.

134

maraca bristle:
bush of thistle threat grizzles —
check before approach.

135

hard growth on pylons,
savage, slice through skin, unmoved,
still hoping for life.

136

foundation crumbling —
flooring falling into swamp —
bamboo on the rise.

137

help me uncover
gashes in the ground from where
ascaris hatches.

138

under warm blanket
of dog, I can allow growth
like greenhouse produce.

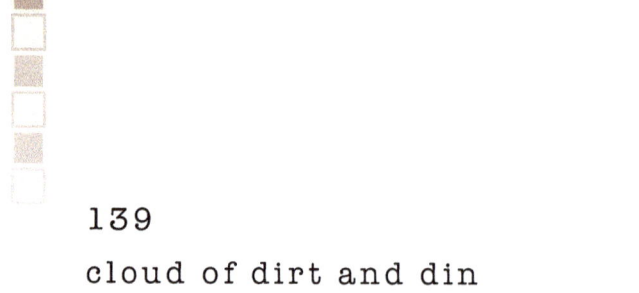

139

cloud of dirt and din
as birdsong splits the morning —
a provocation.

140

hew to heart of wood —
bark hanging off black ash rings —
a tree lain to rest.

141

sucked straw turns to cud —
ruminating on barbed bed,
goat turns head to folk.

142

stream's flow weak, touching
fewer rocks, roots, and runnels —
nature's candlestick.

143

helmeted fungus
thrusts through air from spawn, grouping
amongst hoods in shade.

144

fall onto pillows
of yellow, eyes watering —
no rest for the red.

145

at the heart of trails —
a struggle for coarse or smooth —
hear the wishbone snap.

146

weight of stick digits
blows joints — leaf, limb fall with it —
once high, now grounded.

147

ringing call of bell
brings the cattle home to well —
from graze to shelter.

148

I know who you are
hooting horns to the night like
jazz on frenchmen street.

149

in brisk flit moments
leaves see each other waving
as they fall silent.

150

spines twined as dancers'
arms, their frames unfolding fruit
like loosened proffers.

151

branch drifting downstream,
drowned, water stressed (by own flow) —
guide it with current.

152

there's no darkness here —
just glow of forest smoldered
as rebirth alights.

153

I am but a bee —
bumbling dumb upon blossom's
vibrant open scales.

154

dahlias rise high,
unfurl in a cappella,
and curl as notes fade.

155

torpid volcano
yawns hot breath through ridge to tail,
stirred by nipping shakes.

156

bright hides in skyline —
defined by dark feathered forms
and thin strips of storm.

157

spades and devil's lot —
creeping slow in layman's eyes,
pothos thrives in dark.

158

gem, bright as a gem,
shines through screened dirt, its gleaming
incomparable.

159

cornucopia —
pomegranate, peach, citrus —
shared 'tween lips on isle.

160

a nighttime downpour
captures headlight on windshield,
blinding fractal eyes.

161

sharp lines on pavement
over stilled grass in the night,
give contract in cold.

162

ah, the raven's caw —
stroking shadows, casting light
on settled decay.

163

knitted coverings
clear in cold when stitches shine
in constellations.

164

just for a moment —
glowing in midday sun, leaves
live vivid, then fall.

165

a parched wind exhales,
and curled aspen leaves sigh, each
breath a little death.

166

dreadful heck holds head
like wild ancestor, leering
toward sign of red.

167

ring from the gas lamp —
lighting gravel and failed grass —
cloaking wondrous tree.

168

amaryllis wilts —
rip its heads and let new seeds
form in quiet peace.

169

flagstone pulls apart
atop shifting sediment
from waterfall's flow.

170

a deep quivering
begs and nourishes navel —
tail twitching content.

171

we missed the cold dew —
slept through muddying droplets
as they rolled down leaves.

172

snap the flower stems —
slide them in a vase, save them
before the first freeze.

173

a cracked disc of trunk
holds heavy resting letters
and forest's echoes.

174

drooping — like willow,
we find ease on the streambed —
as days grow shorter.

175

some glass against wind,
I let you in, you breathe leaves
en mi esfera.

176

let's build a stone bridge,
meet where mosses join, and watch
the stream sweep our doubt.

177

carve into hillsides
and lay railroad ties to loot
jet and ore from beast.

178

the elder tree does
not expect saplings to grow
modeled trunk and limbs.

179

the raven may come
by way of peanut trails, or
tilt its head from branch.

180

if I lift rock up,
pulling coarse sides from dirt walls —
I uncover life?

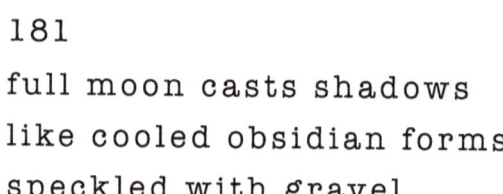

181

full moon casts shadows
like cooled obsidian forms
speckled with gravel.

182

grizzled beast lumbers,
heavy shoulders and low paws
scrape yawning cave mouth.

183

color quilts the ground,
weaving tapestries of time
as trees come to rest.

184

he puffs his feathers,
dances circles on concrete —
asking after nest.

185

I've scraped the bottom
of a bed, raked shovel's spade
on mesh, shaft on bed.

186

don't leave the pepper
to rot or freeze — reap its warmth
by season's slumber.

187

cull the seed to store —
its simple sinless shell clutched
tight 'til cold's closure.

188

watch me as I crack
these rocks open to reveal
ribboned gems within.

189

we see you peeking
'twixt hilltops — cleansing thickets
and destroying death.

190

concrete slab buckles,
pressed hard by root, stricken through
as green finds its way.

191

an other streambed:
here, water polishes stone —
stone husbands water.

192

a dry wind whispers
the stream's timbre through frayed leaves —
changing seasons' chords.

193

no leaf imagines
fall — and when it leaves, it hopes
not to go alone.

194

tear strips from the clouds
let them dissolve in your mouth —
or grant sweet the sky.

195

crushed and split open
on a road of coarse woodgrain —
knife pecking nut guts.

196

accept the tenor
crooning through the barren trees
at summer lust's ease.

197

the yellow season
grays to bone in high desert
as chamisas freeze.

198

under late fall moon —
its crescent cradling venus —
grasses embrace sleep.

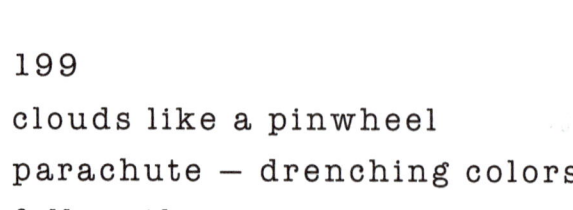

199
clouds like a pinwheel
parachute — drenching colors
fall as the sun sets.

200
frenzied clouds, empty —
silent and pale — shrewd, jeering
fingers choking peaks.

201
a chill wind excites —
slicing through juniper whorls —
catching startled breath.

202

fire breathes in cold air —
tasting raw of bleeding tree —
keeps warm what should freeze.

203

when an ant reaches
its boundary, scent sloughed off,
it might turn or look.

204

it's gutter water —
velvet, painted with rainbow —
meant to mix with oil.

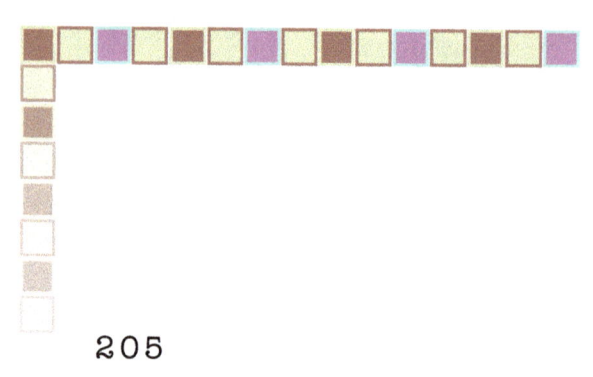

205

infant sparks ringing
over a dusted roadway —
waking pulse of dusk.

206

a leaden drumming —
timber collapsing timber —
stirs groans, squeaks alike.

207

as branches lose leaves,
displaced air takes its home,
swallowing bare space.

208

doorway frozen shut —
exiled ant slogs graveled path —
dead leaves lead the way.

209

lugging bleak boulders —
fixed and stuck with freezing mud —
hatch hides in grayed snow.

210

held between cupped palms —
its wings buffeting our skin —
tickles light as hair.

211

red coop wide open —
an egg left in stingy straw
as hens crowd for warmth.

212

clinging on, high strung
to the topmost branch, a leaf
shivers its last sigh.

213

she found her burrow
two months before I searched — striped
whiptail hibernates.

214

the crow sneaks its food
off asphalt, short hops at chips —
tanged tongue, bouncing quick.

215

frosted mountaintop —
light dusting like eye shadow —
snow sagging branches.

216

pair of pine needles —
split by wind, torn from tree —
unite in crisp snow.

217

the drying thistle
dots our countryside and waits —
ready to storm roads.

218

the mouse finds refuge —
climbing quiet in the night —
gorging on stored food.

219

sheets of spectacles
magnifying beige grasses —
soon to be obscured.

220

be like the piñon:
open even in winter —
spines accepting snow.

221

standing in desert —
sturdy silhouetted limbs —
fading gradient.

222

I smell the bold rain —
creeping through cobwebbed window —
infusing my sleep.

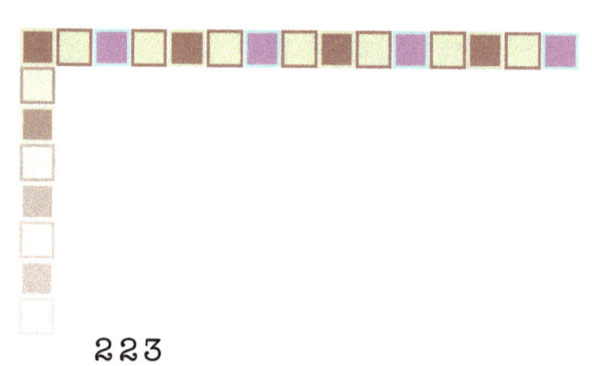

223

waiting for stillness —
splintered moon covered by clouds —
and yet, a slight breeze.

224

lion's shielding roar —
and human doesn't begin
to mouth agape.

225

after sloshed cocoons —
goo like rich guacamole —
butterflies unite.

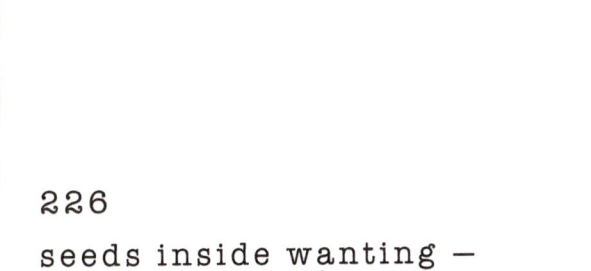

226

seeds inside wanting —
shell clutching closed, being cold —
carry them to spring.

227

a carpenter ant —
maws locked down on withered leaf —
petrification.

228

the snake's brittle molt —
once a set of shielding scales —
notes to grow again.

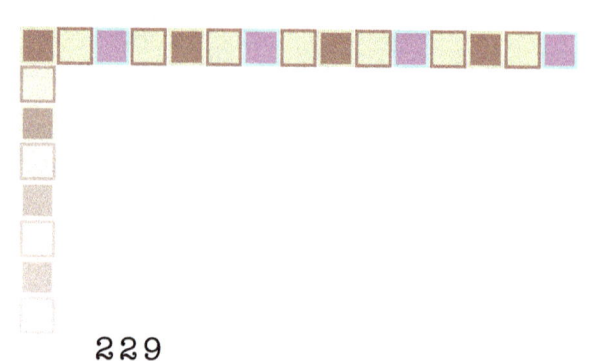

229

she shredded cardboard —
teeth aching in bitter air —
and curled up to sleep.

230

screeching yips at night —
wind-breaking hollow threatened —
loose pairs come to band.

231

pleased by the water —
sitting still in swirled glass cup —
cool and not icy.

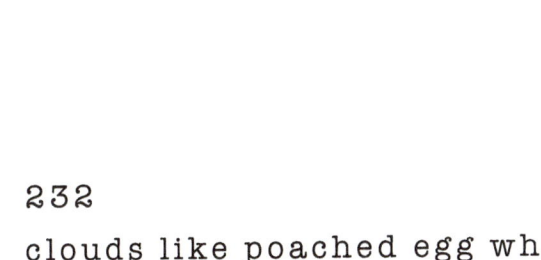

232

clouds like poached egg whites —
chips flaking off in frenzy —
slow quenching cracked earth.

233

casting thin smoke trails —
sparks exploding from hot snaps —
cozy camp's fireworks.

234

the faces in bark —
rugged, deep eyes and split lips —
trail to outstretched limbs.

235

hold my hollow breath —
a child in hibernation,
hunkered for winter.

236

streetlights paint wet roads —
tires grip in December rain —
no danger, no snow.

237

the frost-crusted grass —
crystals hold it still in wind —
ruthless, frozen hugs.

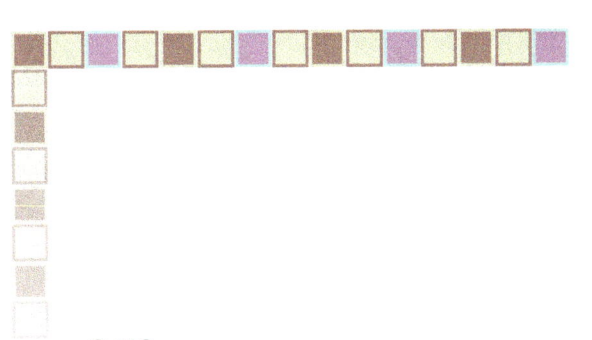

238

in brumal bustling,
fevered tiny creatures blight —
a cold punishment.

239

chilled content water —
clinging still to the pond's banks —
ripples as leaves drop.

240

tired moon has risen,
fallen, watching with cold eyes —
wonder at stubborn.

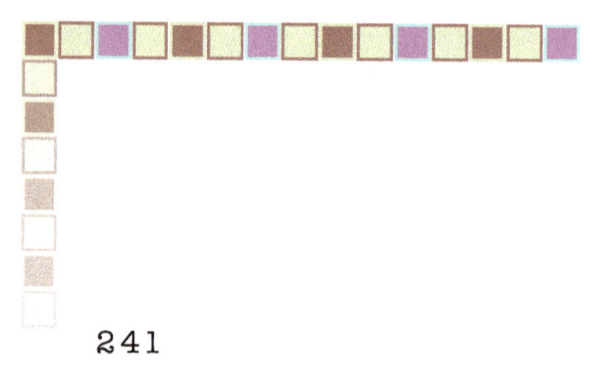

241

a reservoir dried —
the holes in a rain barrel —
bear the single pail.

242

numbed fingers like bulbs —
skin stings on purpled knuckles —
cold pain, do not touch.

243

the moon's longest strides —
wearing its tipped hat of cloud —
halfway to curtain.

244
from the peak, we fall —
avalanche of thawing time —
child sun shines on snow.

245
and we will feel it —
the simple sand in our shoe —
the fire lighting fog.

246
it's not just a jug —
it carries heavy water —
tip it right! don't spill!

247

an ant finds its own
trail helped lead it to the food —
so proud of its role.

248

cold and wearing white
sheets, mountains loom in mourning
at shriveled holly.

249

when you reach the peak —
the coldest and thinnest air —
you create your own.

250

white falling in pitch —
cold wind covers tree branches —
cozy quilt to don.

251

fox's folded ears
pricked with tiny frozen stars —
red diving through banks.

252

an absence of scent —
sucked days before each snowfall —
life retreats for warmth.

253

old, hardened tortoise —
I thought your shell defensive —
instead, it's your home.

254

it's a cold, like snow —
locks us indoors, safe, away,
frozen streets can't meet.

255

look to the flurries
and the snow blown from branches —
uncontrolled chaos.

256

if a leaf returned
to its tree, dried flaws mended —
frosts coax back to ground.

257

understand the stag —
antlers glint mean in moonlight,
sparkle with the snow.

258

time to be like bear —
big, ferocious beast bearing
down on warm slumber.

259

adolescent rift —
a chasm widens, violent —
puzzled cliffs push off.

260

a little longer —
let the snow build pyramids
high on our limbs.

261

a sun takes and gives —
cold wisps swirl, warm bubbles push —
inhale and exhale.

262

the owl's concave eyes,
soaking in each bright twinkle,
lay bare mysteries.

263

echeveria —
fuzzy winter coat prickling —
thick leaves, bundled core.

264

a train of lights rests —
climbing a peaked silhouette —
shine cold through gray haze.

265

ice like a hard seal,
caulking the cracks in asphalt —
sleeping seed beneath.

266

a rock I'm under —
leaving hunched as dirt crumbles —
brisk pricks skin and breathes.

267

mind the ice, a slide —
grabbing, pulling at hoofed feet —
a comical slip.

268
small, stern prairie dog,
sleep clinging to its glazed eyes —
freeze, dog; still winter.

269
moon's diaphragm heaves —
bringing pocked chest to full light —
and recedes in waves.

270
moon aghast, screaming
through thick puffs of ghostly cloud —
a tight, gray aura.

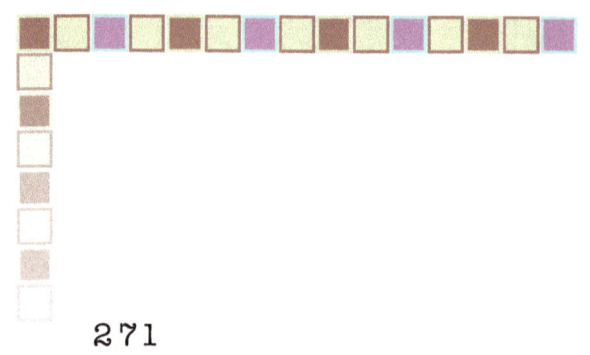

271

clouds sign scared over
swollen, sepia-tone face —
black wick reveals harm.

272

in coldest sunset —
bitter eye squinting at all —
still puffs soften mind.

273

when nothing is seen —
flat, obsidian surface —
icy skate to end.

274

flawless, simple molt —
hair like bumps, cold or afraid —
life leaves unnoticed.

275

it may be the moon —
may be the life it shines through —
look to each in mind.

276

wait ... I have met you —
stallion imposed on sky —
horned espiritu.

277

I see white, orange
spilling across blue canvas —
and cheeks tingle cold.

278

chilled tongue, pinprick flakes —
fresh air ballooning the core —
winter's iron lung.

279

a mid-morning moon —
grin slipping from blue pocket —
cloud hands tickle chin.

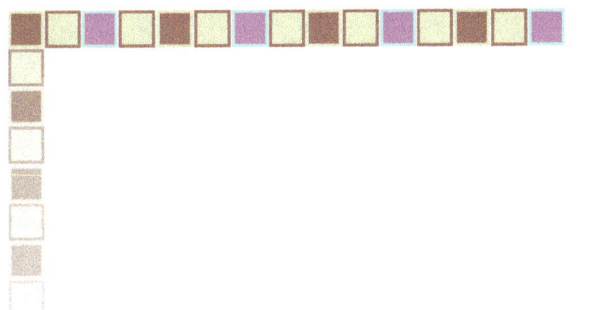

280

dim snow aliens —
shimmering wave in moonlight —
beckon us, we pray.

281

an underground thread —
dormant aspens resonate —
deep hums hugging roots.

282

C. sidhe shimmers green
sitting aside turquoise door —
ghosts fade to firm list.

283

cozy dome of snow —
fractaled feathers propping up
cupped hands, shadows dance.

284

ah, how curious —
seeds sown in fall break through ice —
flaming fingertips.

285

forbidden forrest
[badgers dig tunnels under] —
swooping red egrets.

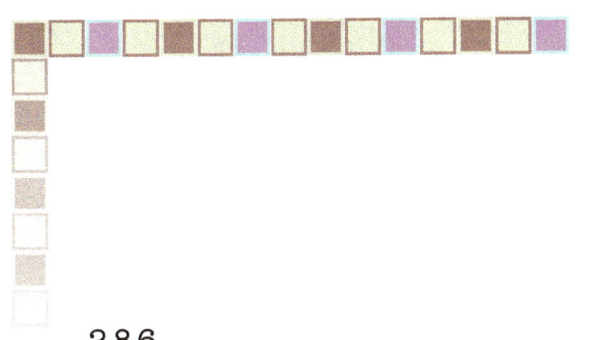

286

in stoney mountains —
shrouded by silencing mist —
music speaks to me.

287

and so, the fellas —
sooted and huddled 'gainst axe —
warmed the ice to melt.

288

a score or more years —
hard frost encases mountains —
shell for growing pains.

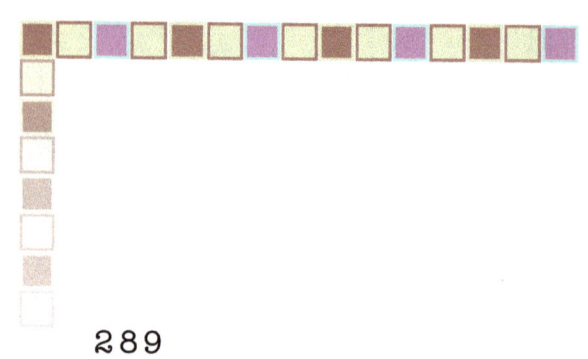

289

fawn traipsing between
pines covered in snow blanket —
circling its wild home.

290

rapid, steaming melt —
straight, often muddied pathways —
glimpses at present.

291

purply green fungus —
shining iridescent like
glimmering treasures.

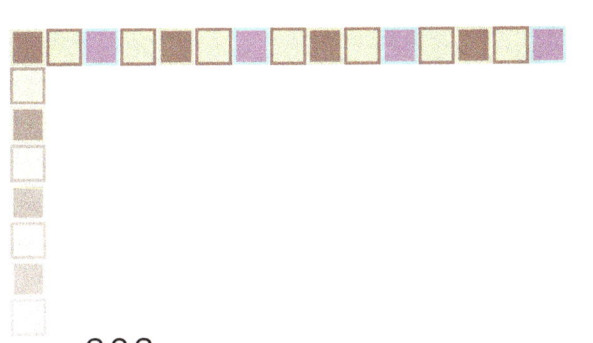

292

a tarantula —
red, hairy legs emerging —
a calm walk from molt.

293

he sits calm in palm —
hooved, red limbs limp with age —
eyes everywhere.

294

at least eight moons shine —
refracted over, over
in light's gushing love.

295
brilliant flashes
as chunks of moon burst apart —
explode hot with love.

296
unique snowflakes pour
forth legions of melting coin —
fluid in moon's bowl .

297
. below, a shower
of sparks like fierce shooting stars —
warm hands grasping, clap.

298
shaking, excited,
a fawn takes its quiet steps —
becoming the stag.

299
beet tugged from floorboards —
tremors and tectonic shifts
break the foundation.

300
el tecolote,
delivering letters high
from above to hart.

301

wrapped in light blanket —
peers out the crystal window —
ancient alliance.

302

hollow ground combusts —
gasses burning off from gates
of deep-ground grand halls.

303

it might be the moon
flooding the bedsheets with light —
calm heads resting soft.

304

glassy Lake Powell —
still, cobalt waters broken
by horrid wasp nest.

305

vibrant black widow —
heater of cold, dark places —
oh, to weave with you.

306

a sled amongst snow —
cold, hardened, its gallant rope
yearns warm, gloved embrace.

307

a city's heartbeat
undulating by its trees —
tire swings sway in breeze.

308

a wind-whipped bushel —
southwest grass tangled hardly —
a complex issue.

309

grand river delta —
mirror rooms of ice reflect —
two dancing currents.

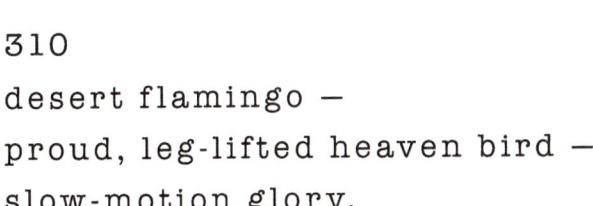

310

desert flamingo —
proud, leg-lifted heaven bird —
slow-motion glory.

311

water street's potholes ...
an erosion of roadways
by torrential rains.

312

eight-legged bastions —
pillars of grace protuding
from soothing, flat pine.

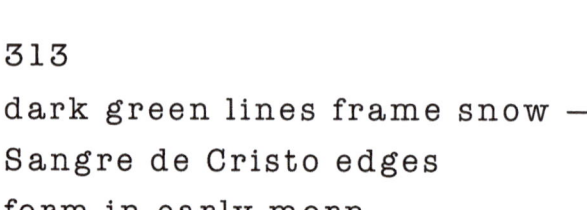

313

dark green lines frame snow —
Sangre de Cristo edges
form in early morn.

314

hear the muted crack!
el pollo loco hatches —
trailing shell and hell.

315

aw, heck! spider does
not see its meandered way
to another's web.

316

I found the north stump —
heart-shaped and thick with fresh moss —
one with which I rest.

317

soft, lemon-peel sky —
morning's scrunching yawns stretch 'cross
Santa Fe heartroads.

318

rolling down hill grass —
hoping the blades don't prickle —
this time I'm ready.

319

brisk rush of spring wind —
moon flower shelters in time —
primed to open fresh.

320

ah! a spider, man!
green-black visage and wicked
patterns in her web.

321

criss cross on a stump
where chainsaw sprayed chunks of flesh
in three awesome bites.

322

it may be the stream
can carry the skipping stone
launched from my side.

323

when the desert sky
loses purple-pastel clouds,
we hope it soon found.

324

and when he — happy,
grizzled bear he is — stretches,
furred eyelids open.

325

petals' shades deepen,
a stark maroon, and bubble
with wilt from snipped stem.

326

I'm about desert
penguins shuffling through thick sand —
wading and waddling.

327

river otter nods —
propelling in white caps, far —
and, grinning, seeks home.

328

I am much obliged
to the well water, its fresh
calcium deposits.

329

in melted puddles
of snow, we see frozen scenes —
stuck and steaming, too.

330

I think we frightened
each other; eight legs might be
better than just two.

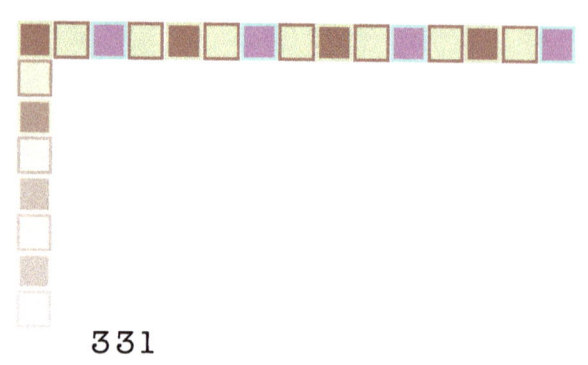

331

a few geniuses
show soft tortoise shell fractals —
solid stills in time.

332

and we wonder how
many corrales mapped our
earth's topography.

333

I see hatred in snow —
wild flurries swipe at my face,
and, still, I see you.

334

they're lost in streetlight —
those pinpricks of fire, seeping
in slow motion at night.

335

we sense root must feel
through atlantis and desert —
a deep-earth radar.

336

cat sees spider nine
times at once — daylight savings'
true treasures, I trust.

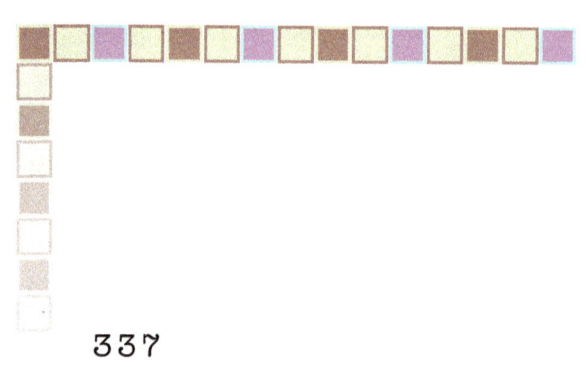

337

at least eighteen steps
set in flagstone — a hopscotch
well worth waiting for.

338

I think ghost insects'
joints creak like weakening wood —
cruel, crunching steps.

339

brown clouds stretch downward —
a light spring of pollution
pockets form letters.

340

a stone can be moved —
its minerals sloughed and smoothed
from a river's mouth.

341

somehow, al alba
begins before the sunrise —
its purples hew skies.

342

thick smoke dissipates —
like burnt smolders in mountain
forrest — rubber trees.

343

solid, gentle hail —
reminder of our dented
tin, its blemishes.

344

thunks on the hardwood
forest — pounding earthen sound
branches hear, and smile.

345

I see bulbous fangs —
fresh fear feathering vision —
I cup your body.

346

I think when we found
a stump — its cuts worn — we heard
each ole street's heartbeat.

347

when we think it's not —
snow covering grass in spring —
it comes up harder.

348

snake alley's snow melts —
its wild brush, gray with death, turns
up to the spring sun.

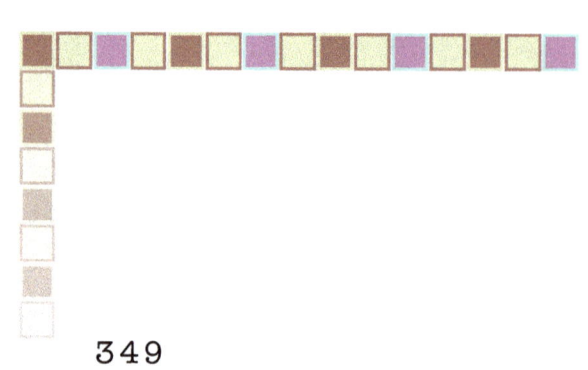

349

maybe at night, bats —
in the dark caves of Carlsbad —
are drawn by bright beams.

350

the pigeon shits, yet
we know it's spring by the bird's
brilliant refrain.

351

baby elephant —
telephone-pole limbs muddied —
mother's calls clog ears.

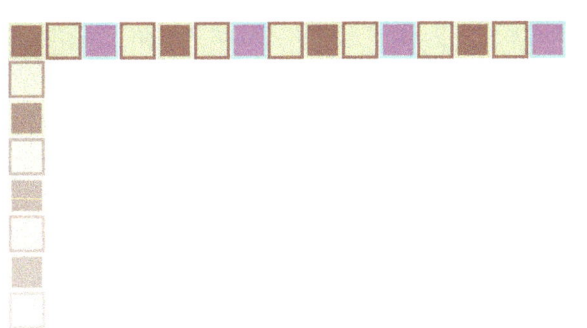

352

tongue the molasses —
its sweet expulsion from deep —
speech, a trickled treat.

353

these are not your leaves —
would I could suspend from limbs,
let them lie — sprout, child.

354

the cracked, droughted earth
needs only small hands to crush
it back to sand, dirt.

355

deep in the forest,
you may find trees' hearts scrawled
on splintered stumps — speech.

356

explore connections —
spectrum of deep hues bridging
clouds at sun's rise, fall.

357

delight in water —
color seeps in the twinning
rivers on surface.

358

give with tender care —
the grains inside kept cool, dry
under cushioned bark.

359

a snake's scales do shed —
their shine having grown crusted —
an age over, poached.

360

a gray-green cocoon —
its soupy film falls away—
¡ay, mariposa!

361

wonder when a tree
becomes a story — and where
its roots could have grown.

362

los ojos como
butterflies, and thought flutters—
¡ay, mariposas!

363

frogs' silent lilies —
passing through like gondolas —
sturdy bones alive.

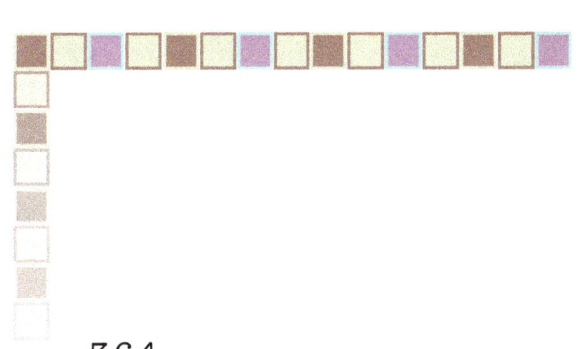

364

these rocks, enchanted —
a sun purple to orange —
reverse gradients.

365

pow! with pale lilac,
clear-violet amethyst
pops to woodgrain heart.

366

no one expectant —
butterflies erupt in green
—paint, mask for my voice.

367

only magic in
one bloom's fortified petals —
loose like purple scarves.

368

a clover, its four
leaves shining gold in early
dew's dawning prism.

369

even in a drought —
a trickle at best, thin blood,
thin bone — river's there.

370

and soon, with thunder —
a rush of breath blessings, and
rains flood arroyos.

371

pink moon washes o'er —
silent blossoms flowing — stream
carries them to rest.

372

though even petals —
soft and streaked, shining in sun —
might block a stream's path.

373

take a twig and swirl —
clear the eddies and embrace
the sun's glittering.

374

view the place, sacred
maze of bladed geode green
and shimmering gold.

375

thick, hefty breathing —
wind billows tendrils to clouds —
heat choking birdsong.

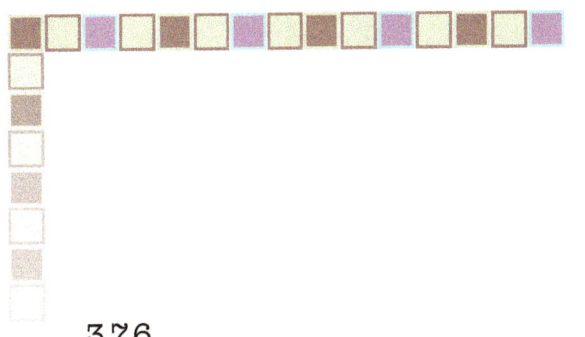

376

see the sun saw through —
as orange and purple hewed,
flames fade; growth anew.

377

dried leaves, better brought
to heat in slow simmering —
steam supple petals.

378

see smoke's streams, incensed —
rolling ripples in water —
and dance, reach for rain.

379

as fog's fingers lift,
rising in early morning,
streaked lotus opens.

380

brisk night under moon —
a tipped chalice accepting
the sun's heated wax.

381

its pale stems meeting
the sun — shadows lifting sloughed
scales, colors to sage.

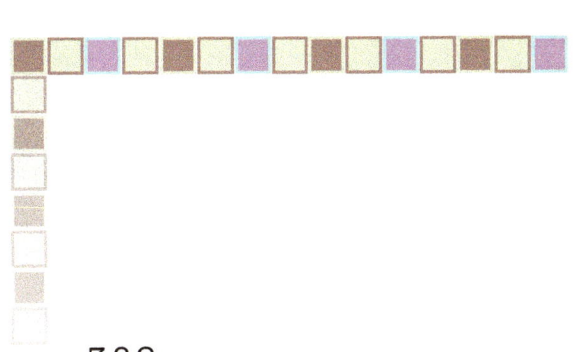

382

light breeze breathes, lilting —
a lily's head, shriveled. light
the sun; heavy the rain.

383

maybe the tree sleeps
under its canopy's shade —
leaves blacking out the sun.

384

kneel at mauve aster —
count its petals, brush its style —
cherish its nature.

385

could be creosote
or watered oil on asphalt —
humid air incense.

386

you are the sky orb,
orange — and when the tendrils
clear, a twinkling star.

387

in flux be the moon —
waxing and wanting, waning
and wondering. flux.

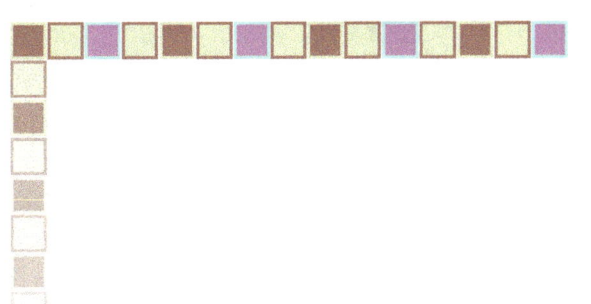

388

two halves an earth there;
we could do with two suns, tear —
by gravity — walls.

389

the sand on the beach —
powerful vibrations shift
it in stacked patterns.

390

meet where minerals
from the cliffs mix with soft grains
of sand at the shore.

391

hope to see a cloud —
breathe and see it dissipate —
rain mist to our trees.

392

see sparks like fireflies —
cotton puffs catching sunlight —
vitreous visions.

393

water veins crawling
up hillsides, reaching for more —
pigments crying out.

394

flower moon calls us —
a gathering of clouds, cool
and collecting rain.

395

how can we translate
the winds' gushing or silence —
give us nature's key.

396

sense the branch you reach
for — its joints and foliage;
know its strong support.

397

the morning crawls like
silver fish over mountains,
cascades to valleys.

398

moon brushes bright dust
into the night, sprinkling earth's
pull with spirit motes.

399

pinch down at the base —
knuckle and thumb locking stem;
tug. dirt sprays, roots tear.

400

pale white gleams in beads —
stars hold dollops of water
as dawn breaks the night.

401

the last breaths of trees
embed in brethren by steam —
pass by piñon past.

402

even a clear sky —
unpainted by pastel clouds —
hosts the sun's passion.

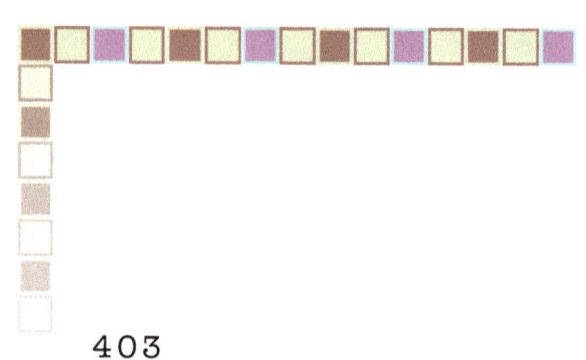

403

walk into the wind —
cotton clumps clamor, brushing
face for attention.

404

the ground, it— the ground
rain high at the struggling clouds —
thunder dirt— light crowns.

405

the sun like sheep's wool —
eyes closed, cheek kissed by cool dawn —
take time to rake rock.

406

the horizon gleams,
its new day bursting with green —
chilled and smokeless rays.

407

come nude to the world —
pale blade of grass, easily
bent by foot or breeze.

408

crave the icicle —
steady drip refracting beams,
pooling cool on tongue.

409

see the slate frozen —
a dented disc slowly turns
gold by fixed starlight.

410

I pluck mulberry
from the sky, cloud by cloud 'til
the sun is risen.

411

little apricot —
nestled deep in black velvet
sheets, pocked and glowing.

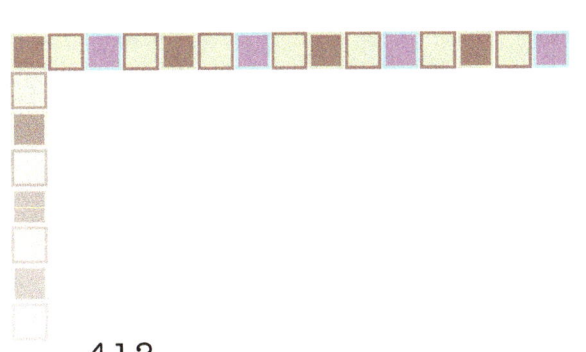

412

see the silhouette —
its rigid form caught in clouds,
a white blackhole ring.

413

gather the hot stones —
their ribbons and ridges shine
with each moon movement.

414

lift cragged monoliths —
six feet, carried long distance
to your hilly home.

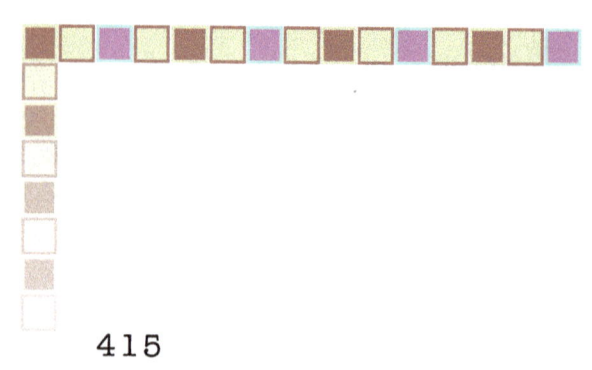

415

shatter the glassy
black: rain bullets slug puddles;
lightning splits thick clouds.

416

sandpaper windshield —
a thousand and one lights catch
my eye — wiped away.

417

twisted cloud fortune —
sun's last minute highlights gold
in foothills' creases.

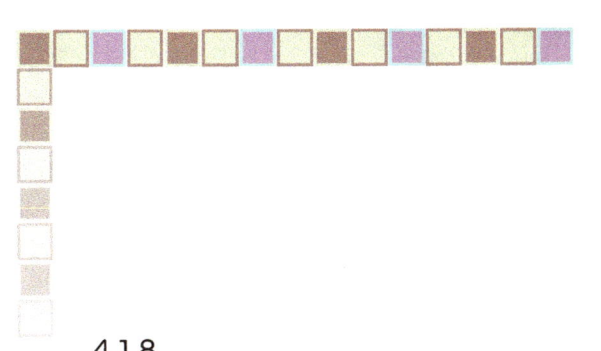

418

when a fly tickles
your ear, open a window —
listen to the trees.

419

dew drops on rhythm —
dawn draws the grass harmonics —
sit still, let it soak.

420

dripping hot, honey
steams into swirl and vapor —
warmed oil on soaked road.

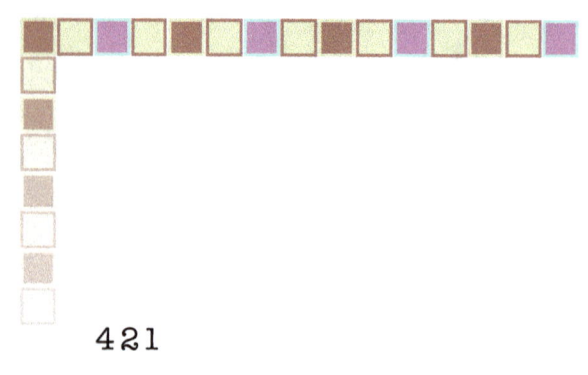

421

turtle's eternal
expansion — it may see moss
like rainforest rocks.

422

pink-ribboned orchid,
flourishing by slow-warmed ice —
petals thick and soft.

423

one day to be stone —
some sides smooth, others ridged with
infinite crumble.

424

two days to be breeze —
rapping the door, asking for
humble home to fill.

425

three days to be flame —
fluid dancer sponging air,
freestyle warmth and flare.

426

four days to be rain —
cool sheets resting eyes, passing
nights, noons drip by drop.

427

like dancing ashes,
cotton flurries mingle 'mongst
the summer beetles.

428

legs like jellyfish
ribbons flying across gold
sunbeams: mosquito.

429

folded-steel lightning
booms through pitched clouds — slicing eyes —
and I sit, legs crossed.

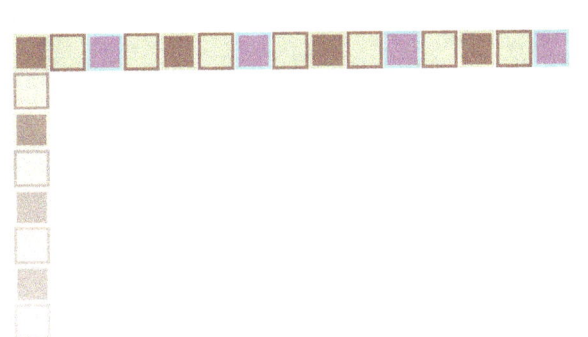

430

ridged and slate, round stone
like a plate — its divet filled
with a placid flood.

431

lone flower floating
across the wild, empty blue —
what shapes tomorrow?

432

roadsides are loaded —
clover grasses, we wonder
at our cushioned soles.

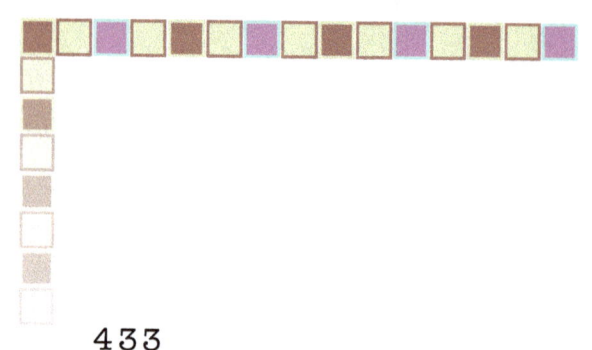

433

shed the shrouded mists —
we kiss seasoned horns goodbye,
ask buck moon's new shine.

434

I suppose the bird,
humming drunkenly, sipped from
agave's flower.

435

I'll not sing for you —
this whistle, these warbles (mine!),
are for just the peace.

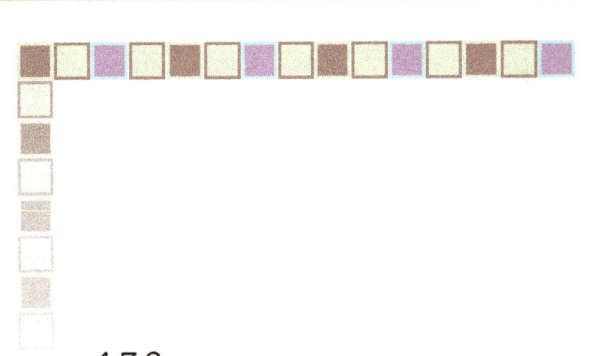

436

hide in a crevice —
flicker in the glowing lights —
flutter by eyesight .

437

mixing snipped flowers —
matching bouquets to nineties
jukebox dancing jams.

438

born from fire's frenzy.
with what luck that wood should float,
same with that it burns.

439

salt tightens my tongue —
hot dough risen, pressed by thumb —
gentle pretzel gift.

440

when winter's fingers
release bark under snow moon,
the trees crack from cold.

441

flower corona —
petals ringing in sunlight,
leaves play the wind's chords.

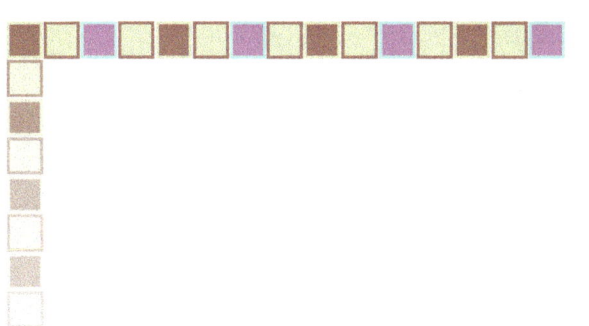

442

cat kneads sun's beams —
the lazy spring afternoon
invites a light breeze.

443

a flower stem's hairs,
steeping in the springtime sun,
like lemon rooibos.

444

one by one, dry dust
star particles burst — rupture
in shimmering life.

445

in a frothing stream,
each rushing bubble vibrates —
voices echo air.

446

follow the fungi —
orange branches crawl along
log, rock, and root veins.

447

its sunmost ledges
give great green grins, the mountain
exhales soft with moss.

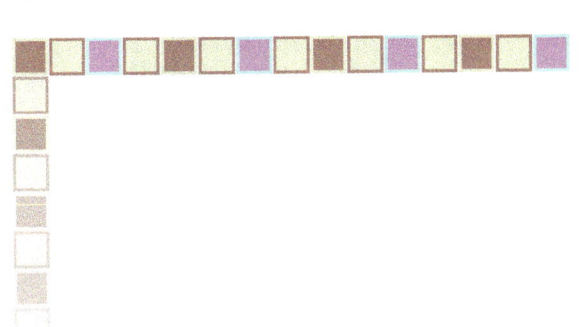

448

a caramel scent
caught and whisked upon the wind —
bees drone to their home.

449

sky illusionists
(clouds swim in many shaded
shoals) — everchanging.

450

sand shoals shift over
hungry lands, sifting their grains
on earth's stomate pores.

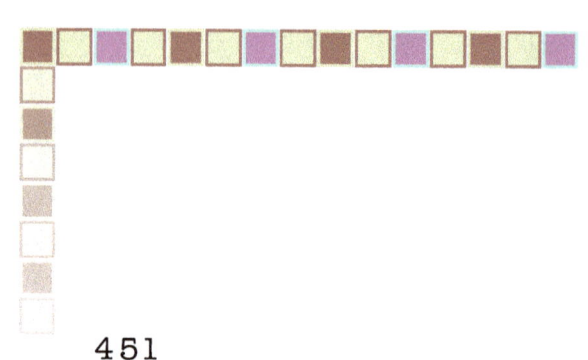

451

mountain hills covered
in green, mossy fir, hazy
or sharpened by wind.

452

see the fog like breath —
white caps blooming from the pine —
a shared rise and fall.

453

open a window —
moonlight breeze through budding trees —
the spring's anxious voice.

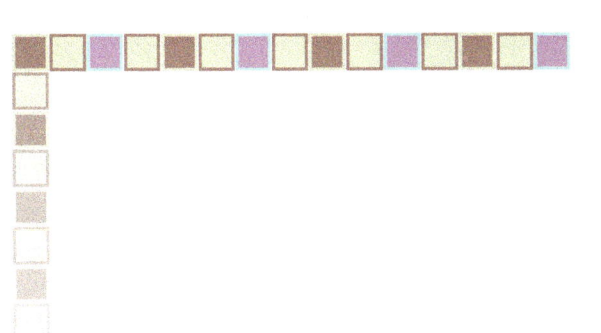

454

the sun cracks like yoke —
its rays spilling through tree tops,
birthing a new day.

455

clouds over mountain —
the strong pinnacle breaking
from desert's body.

456

air imbues its breath —
an energy for sages
lining the rolled hills.

457

the breeze a strong push —
the same energy as sways
cornstalks in their dance.

458

waterfall faces
form with the passing of time —
fuzzy like cotton.

459

petals leaving life —
wilting fabrics of color
quilting to the wind.

460

glowing limbs beckon
attention — a peacocking
coral preening eyes.

461

energy vessel —
grains of sand pile in the core —
turn, turn to relieve.

462

stone on the mountain —
two widow bites to index
on the mountain's head.

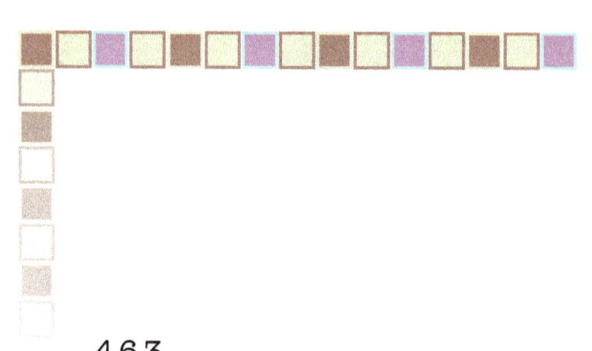

463

follow the cold creek
where mountain shade turns spring green
and fuzzy with birth.

464

stretched strands of lightning
pull cotton-layered lattice
into monsoon pours.

465

the petals open —
tight spirals undulating
in summer sundance.

466

cloud like metallic
grin on the sun's burning face
morphs to furrowed brows.

467

build on a boulder
whose highest hilltop hails health
to the sun's energy.

468

remember the ants —
they grapple with human grains —
otherwise and thoughts.

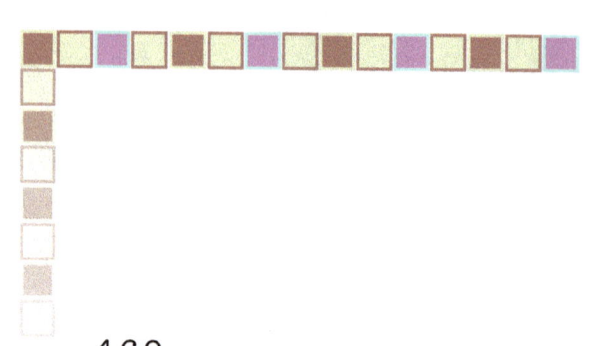

469

we hold butterflies —
our fingers like stems whose prints
unfurl in petals.

470

evergreen mountain,
speckled yellow with freckles,
beckons fellow grins.

471

standing with the winds —
breath from autumn heckles leaves
ready to return.

472

listen! trampled dirt
grapples footstep's massive girth —
monsoons clap back — earth!

473

flow with breeze which moves
through trees — dance of leaves like dog's
whirlwind on toe beans.

474

stars collide in pitch —
pinpricks of energy rays
raining down to earth.

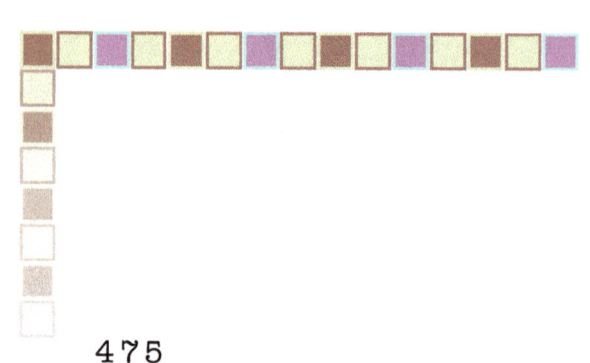

475

light the sacred herbs!
breathe deep the earth's ground presence!
rejoice 'round the flame!

476

quilted fire ahead —
sky alight with day's closing —
roasting with passion.

477

snow encapsulates —
rigid flakes falling to set
a morning indoors.

478
I see no blue skies —
only falling clouds — a rush
of infinite gray.

479
snow melt leaves dry leaves
dancing to crow's caws — cold calls,
beckons winter storm.

480
no flicker alike —
no crack, snap, or pop can ring
alone in the dark.

481

dust angels swirling —
leaves caught in godly twirling —
this way and that way.

482

just a rock, painted
over and over — varied
angles of scrawled cracks.

483

each unique snowflake
melts into puddle's 'moebic,
grave infinity.

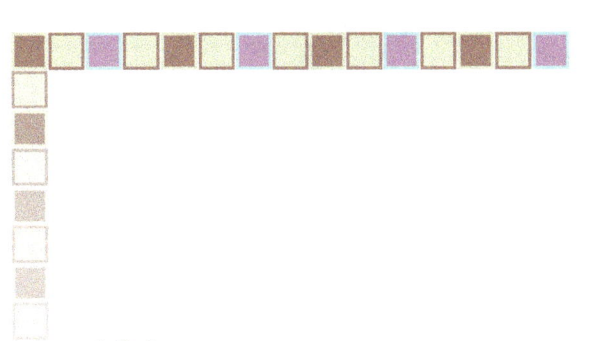

484

icicles melting —
each sun-boiled drop a free
soul to rejoin dirt.

485

earth is a pock-marked
face with sea eyes, volcano
white heads, a tree beard.

486

cloud wisps pink in blue —
a moment of solitude
strung by morning light.

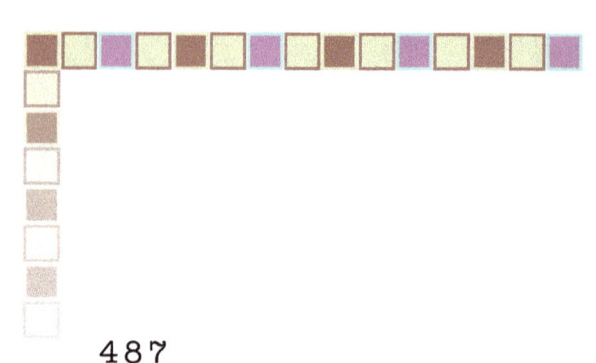

487

fog, the breath of trees,
rests in the nighttime streetlights —
carrying snowflakes.

488

we grow toward the sun —
and return to earth as earth,
to grow again new.

489

ashen clouds shifting,
stirred by moonlit concerto
playing on the wind.

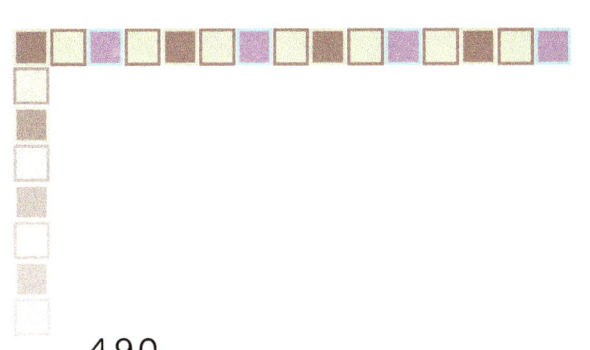

490

cold as winter stone —
a boulder to behold in
sunlight's warm prayers.

491

an infant flower,
I stretch petals — finding where
air gives its support.

492

no shortage of stone,
the mountains offer perches
for the divine winds.

493

waves of steam erupt
as flame and stream meet their birth —
energy's ebb, flow.

494

as I sit barren —
wind tickles hairs on my legs
and my rivened lungs.

495

deciduous stands
half aglow in winter sun —
golden light of God.

496

solace in silence —
snow joins steam over brewed tea,
jasmine in blizzard.

497

glistening eye stars
falling from lashes in warm
fractal-formed crystals.

498

dawn light brightest 'pon
storm's snowy dusk and coldest
glints in blue-eyed morn.

499

dropped grapes for the crow —
guardian of the daytime,
warrior of night.

500

stony precipice,
the standing mount for cawing
sermons and raised hair.

501

clouds gather in mist —
breathless in the cold, snow chokes
winter nights quiet.

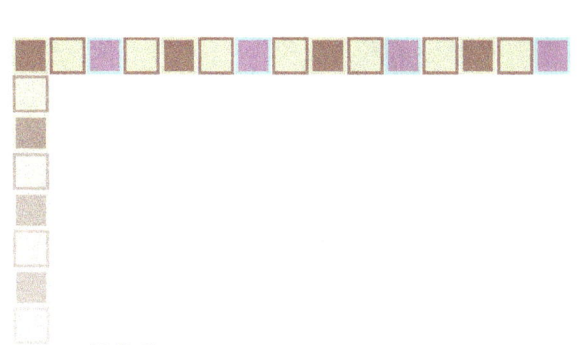

502

trees with one thousand
and one barren twigs and white-
lined branches — waiting.

503

icicles on hare —
king cloaked in winter's silver
shares the open light.

504

broken a moment,
dawn frost's quiet returns from
crow caws as moon sets.

505

satisfied desert
in el niño's gatherings —
winter comes with gifts.

506

time frozen as fish
leaps from stream, maw outstretched, claw
sharp in free air — drop.

507

passionflower swirls —
striped petals, static spirals
in beholden wind.

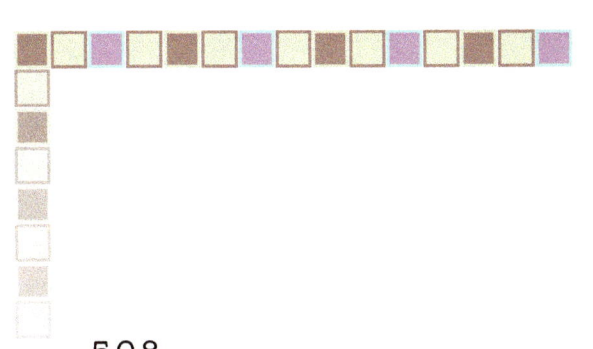

508

god of beginnings
reigns thirty-one days, even
through frozen blossoms.

509

I like clouded wisps
lit by a wax moon — I like
when the ants walk by.

510

wind like violin
bows across prairie sky blades —
sunset sonata.

511

veil of limb and cloud —
silver smile bright shining through,
marriage to wolf moon.

512

the great thief rotates
earth's cycles like petals fall
and curl and wrought life.

513

creatures of darkness
whisper and scream as if night
is light — and it is.

514

dirt forgives trees their
fallen leaves, knowing each brings
rich spring borne to earth.

515

today we feel fright
as if some eight legs could step
harder than our two.

516

grapes left for raven
taken by ravenous child —
learn to leave it be.

517

dried flowers like stained
glass panes bring winter colors
into our body.

518

behold, the beauty
swirls in dawn's pinpricks sifting
slow through frozen trees.

519

quiet night splitting
by winter wind's roar through limbs —
leaves' restless mem'ry.

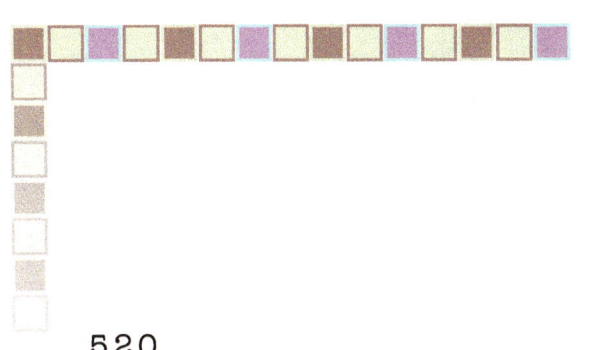

520

a simple stillness,
a double sunset — colors
giving life meaning.

521

to sit is to watch
a cloud or feel the wind, hear
a crow or to sit.

522

I am a straw bale —
pushed twig to twig and strung
tight by the two twine.

523

when a droplet hits
still water, still water must
learn to accept it.

524

here now, shadows cast
long and short in a timelapse
quick as breath, slow spring.

525

oh, orion, please
don't leave as the seasons change —
guard my sky each night.

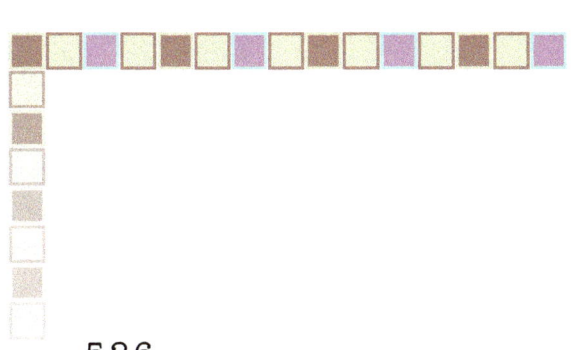

526

be my orange moon
reflecting the sun back in
the night, my daylight.

527

birds expect chorus
when wind blows through the spring buds —
vivid death made life.

528

what cuts the fiber
of each leaf in autumn time
chooses the leaves' rot.

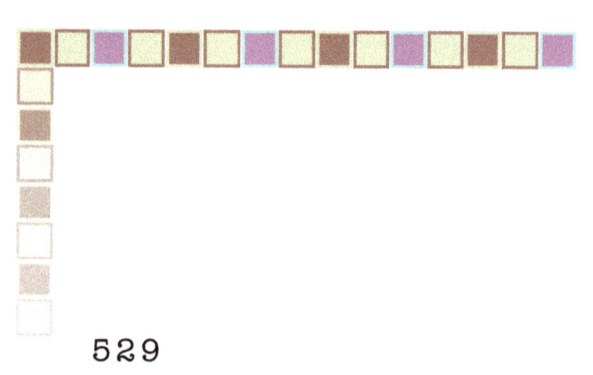

529

the moon half alight,
pulled by the earth, hangs balanced
by sun's burning might.

530

overcast or clear, sun
shines somewhere; caring for your
own seed, sun shines there.

531

today, as I sat
in smoke, the wind roared and filled
my space with heaven.

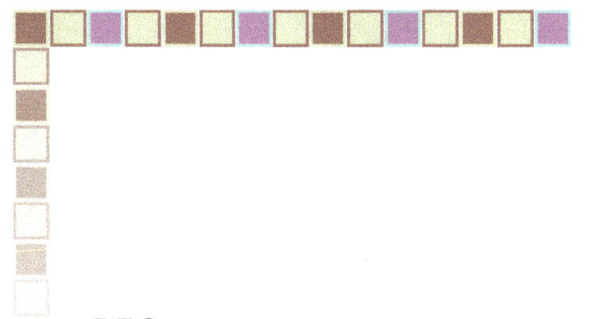

532

not every leaf
falls from the tree; some rattle
as spring breathes back green.

533

listen to the mad
wind, count each hard gasp, and look
for the split sunshine.

534

dry sand grain blasted
from palm to meet the ocean
in a lightning storm.

535

no mistake is made
as sun rises and sets, as
beasts complete their lives.

536

still stream still flows quite
like the calm breath of a monk
sitting amongst sage.

537

open like daisies
to the hazy morning sun —
crowd of bright blossoms.

538

if one waterfall
does not resonate with you,
move up or down stream.

539

violent ruptures
of wind still carry petals
from where to somewhere.

540

the moon studies you —
an ebb and flow of your blood —
as you gaze at it.

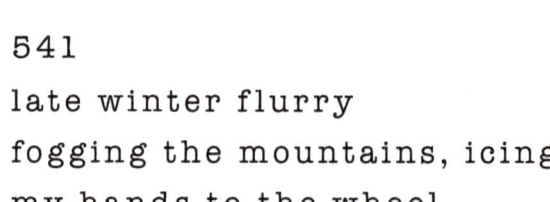

541

late winter flurry
fogging the mountains, icing
my hands to the wheel.

542

carnations in bloom,
a cyclical calling to
spring's buzzing modem.

543

the bees awakening
with pollination sickles
dance in limerance.

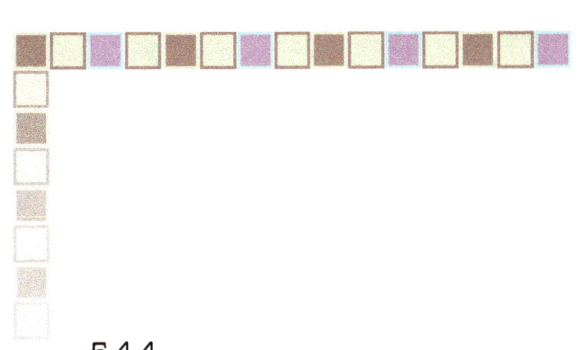

544

we are all flowers —
daisies, roses, and tulips —
blooming and wilting.

545

tumble in pollen —
bee in blooms, jumping rainbow
to rainbow — spring lust.

546

I wait in darkness
for snow's covered compassion
and the bright dawn's light.

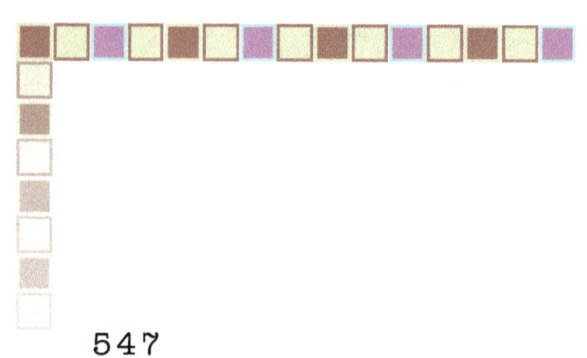

547

between two stone banks
flows a stream moving faster
even when frozen.

548

wind walks over grass —
moving blade to blade until
it's swept far away.

549

bunching fabric clouds
stitched by rain await the spring —
equinox unfolds.

550

flowers on hi-hat —
trees on bass — as the grass rifts
on a springtime gale.

551

I scared the shit out
of two raccoons, or they me
by curiousness.

552

a bamboo thicket
bore wind's chime to our senses,
and we sang our songs.

553

maybe butterflies
carry seeds like we carry
and propagate thought.

554

prairie dog cackles
on its dirt castle as cars
sit in wait, trundle.

555

a silhouette veil
bares the sun and the moon, yet
from its peak, we see.

556

we are the hotsprings
melting minerals in mind —
feel the grit disperse.

557

voices on the breeze —
feather against leaves; what does
present offer thee.

558

waste not majestic
stones, nor trees giving birds home —
waste not day nor night.

559

raw lines of lightning
fill cloud-scuttled sky — I know
I am not alone.

560

the grass is the grass;
when wind blows, the grass does sway —
mostly, it's just grass.

561

pileus halo
of cloud holds the sunlight like
refracting diamonds.

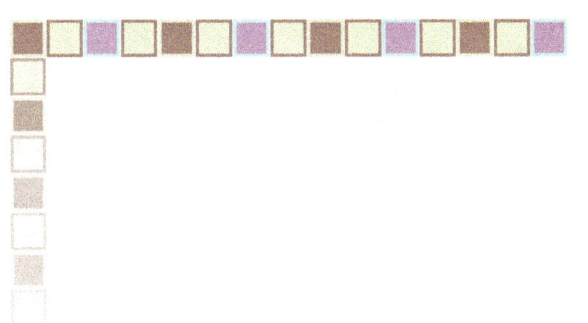

562

searching for sangha
like formidable aspen
roots hold trunks through storm.

563

a kindness in death:
if leaves' rot composts for spring,
their souls must also.

564

a delicate dance
working shadows into moons,
waking all to see.

565

each step brings summit;
each new bud on a waking
tree draws a deep breath.

566

where petals fall, see
their placement and vivid stripes —
a pathway revealed.

567

white petals dancing;
fresh buds on tree's warming twigs
like silly faces.

568

the great moon basket,
full with earth's heavy shadow,
carries many stars.

569

long, vagus pathways
strewn with rot and bloom alike;
the seasons' teachings.

570

ladybugs — rare red
dew drops raising spring's eyelids
like velvet carpet.

571

a crackling as flames
waxed and waned, bright as the moon
in its blue covers.

572

fathom the sky's moon
as clouds waft us the cherry
blossoms' sweet perfume.

573

relative to earth —
its stones and oceans — to ants,
relative to all.

574

glistening gold cap
breathing mycelium waves —
expressing in spores.

575

a bliss in simple
structures nature strings along
with quatrained restraint.

576

Yah heyana-ha
hey-nahana yah
oh n'yana hey-yah.

www.ingramcontent.com/pod-product-compliance
Lightning Source LLC
Chambersburg PA
CBHW071116160426
43196CB00013B/2586